The Trouble With Secrets

Written by Karen Johnsen
Illustrated by Linda Forssell

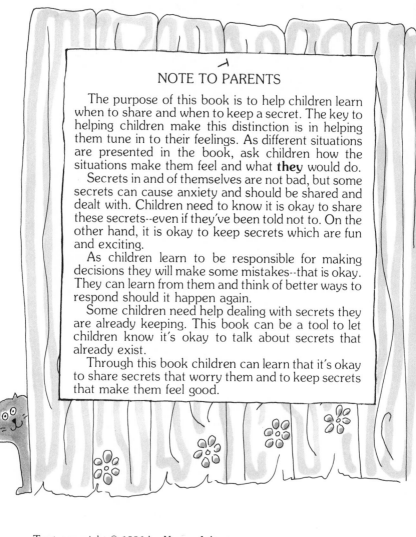

NOTE TO PARENTS

The purpose of this book is to help children learn when to share and when to keep a secret. The key to helping children make this distinction is in helping them tune in to their feelings. As different situations are presented in the book, ask children how the situations make them feel and what **they** would do.

Secrets in and of themselves are not bad, but some secrets can cause anxiety and should be shared and dealt with. Children need to know it is okay to share these secrets--even if they've been told not to. On the other hand, it is okay to keep secrets which are fun and exciting.

As children learn to be responsible for making decisions they will make some mistakes--that is okay. They can learn from them and think of better ways to respond should it happen again.

Some children need help dealing with secrets they are already keeping. This book can be a tool to let children know it's okay to talk about secrets that already exist.

Through this book children can learn that it's okay to share secrets that worry them and to keep secrets that make them feel good.

Text copyright © 1986 by Karen Johnsen
Illustrations copyright © 1986 by Linda Forssell

Parenting Press, Inc.   ISBN 0-943990-22-x
7744 31st Ave NE   ISBN 0-943990-23-8 (lib. binding)
Seattle, WA 98115   LC 85-51803

dedicated to...
Jill
Wendy
AMY
and
Laila

The trouble with secrets is knowing when to share them, when to keep them, and who to share them with.

If a secret worries you or hurts you inside, you need to tell the secret to someone who will listen and help you.

2

If you feel good about a secret, keep it until the right time to share it.

3

If you borrow your daddy's tools and hurt yourself, don't keep it a secret. Even if you think Daddy might get mad at you for using his tools, tell him right away. He might need to take you to the doctor or give you a bandage.

4

If you buy a present for your mommy, keep what is in the present a secret till she opens it. Then she'll be surprised.

If you break Mom's favorite vase, don't keep it a secret.
Even if you glue it back together you need to tell her before
she pours water into the vase.

If you want to surprise your daddy with a batch of chocolate chip cookies, keep it a secret. Wait till after dinner and then surprise him. He'll probably give you a hug.

If somebody hurts you, don't keep it a secret. Even if they warn you not to tell anybody, you need to talk to someone you trust. You can try your mom or dad or your teacher. They can help you find ways to be safe.

8

If you bake muffins with a surprise spoonful of jelly inside, keep it a secret. Wait till someone takes a bite. Then it will be a surprise.

9

If your mommy or daddy gives you medicine or vitamins, that's okay. But if someone else offers you pills to take when you aren't sick, don't take the pills. Don't keep the secret. The pills could make you sick.

If you know the hiding place for the key to your home, keep it a secret! That way you and your family can get into your house when it's locked, but nobody else can find the key.

11

If a big person helps you at bath time, that is okay. But if the washing makes you feel confused or bad, that is not okay. You can tell good touches from bad touches. Don't keep bad touches a secret. Say "NO!" Tell someone that will listen. They'll protect you.

If you know where a bird's nest is, keep it a secret. Then you'll help the mommy bird protect her baby birds.

If you take something without asking, don't keep it a secret. Even if you just borrow something, you need to let the person know and return it right away.

If you know the password to your clubhouse, keep it a secret. Share it with people in your club or friends that plan to join.

If someone offers you a treat to go with them, don't keep it a secret. Say "NO!" and run away. Tell a grown-up who can help, as soon as you can.

16

If you go to a magic show and you see how the magician does the trick, keep it a secret! Then someday you can do the magic trick yourself and surprise everyone.

Your mom might tell you that you're going to have a new baby in your family. If she asks you to keep it a secret, that's okay. She'll let you know when it's okay to share. After awhile everyone can guess anyway.

If a doctor needs to examine you with your clothes off and your parent is there, that's okay. But if anyone wants you to take your clothes off or touch you in an uncomfortable way, that is not okay. Don't keep it a secret! You need to say, "No! I'll tell!" Then run away and tell a grown-up you trust. They'll protect you and help you feel better.

If one of your parents shares secrets with you and tells you not to tell your other parent, that's confusing. If it worries you and you don't understand, let them both know. Tell them how hard it is for you and that you wish they wouldn't tell you things or do things they don't want you to share. Talk to your grandma or grandpa or an auntie or a friend about how you feel. They can help you.

If you know the special ending to a story, keep it a secret. Wait till your friend has finished hearing the story. Then you can share your fun in knowing how the story ended with your friend.

21

The important thing about secrets is learning when to keep them and when to share them.

When a secret worries you or makes you hurt inside, you need to share the secret. Keep telling the secret until someone listens. Then you will feel better.

When you feel good about a secret, it is okay to keep it. Wait until just the right moment and then share your secret. If you tell a good secret too soon, you might spoil the fun.

You can learn when to share secrets and when to keep them.

What would you do if your friend calls and says he's giving your brother a surprise birthday party and wants you to keep it a secret? Would you tell him? Why?

What would you do if your friends started playing with matches and fireworks and asked you to keep it a secret? Would you tell? Why?

25

Remember, the important thing about secrets is deciding whether you should share them or not. If you feel hurt or confused, tell a grown-up you trust. Keep telling until someone listens. If you feel happy and excited, keep the secret until it is time to tell. Then don't be surprised if you get a special hug and smile right back.

Books to Help Protect Children

MY Body ■ A book to teach young children how to resist uncomfortable touch.
Cuerpo Es MIO ■ Spanish translation of *It's MY Body.*
otect Your Child ■ Offers specific activities for children that reduce the likelihood of abuse.
e Trouble With Secrets ■ Helps young children decide whether to keep or share a secret.
ving Touches ■ A book for young children about positive, nurturing touch.
mething Is Wrong At My House ■ A book for children about parents' fighting.
mething Happened and I'm Scared to Tell ■ A book for young victims of sexual abuse.
ping Abused Children ■ A book for those who work or live with sexually abused children.
Kid's Guide to First Aid ■ Lifesaving skills for children 4-12 years old.

ORDER FORM

A Kid's Guide to First Aid	$4.95	___	Trouble With Secrets $3.95	___
Something Is Wrong...	$3.95	___	It's MY Body $3.95	___
Something Happened...	$3.95	___	Loving Touches $3.95	___
Helping Abused Children	$6.95	___	Mi Cuerpo Es MIO $3.95	___
			Protect Your Child $5.95	___

Subtotal _____

Name _____

Shipping _____

Tax (WA add 8.1%) _____

Address _____

Total _____

City _____

State/zip _____

Order subtotal	Shipping
$ 0-$10	add 2.00
$10-$25	add 3.00
$25-$50	add 4.00

Send to: Parenting Press, Inc; P.O.Box 15163, Dept. 600; Seattle, WA 98115